SEAN McGRAIL

ANCIENT BOATS

SHIRE ARCHAEOLOGY

2

Cover illustration
Gold model boat of the first century BC from Broighter,
County Derry, Northern Ireland.
(Copyright: National Museum of Ireland.)

Published by
SHIRE PUBLICATIONS LTD
Cromwell House, Church Street, Princes Risborough,
Aylesbury, Bucks, HP17 9AJ, UK.

Series Editor: James Dyer

ISBN 0 85263 626 1

First published 1983

Set in 11 point Times roman and printed in Great Britain by
C. I. Thomas & Sons (Haverfordwest) Ltd,
Merlins Bridge, Haverfordwest.

Contents

Acknowledgements

I am grateful to James Dyer, Veryan Heal and Anne McGrail who read the first draft of this book and made many useful suggestions, and to the Trustees of the National Maritime Museum for permission to publish many of the illustrations. All illustrations are National Maritime Museum copyright unless otherwise stated in the caption.

Note

Prehistoric dates in this text are approximate and are given in calendar years. The books mentioned in Further Reading give the radiocarbon and other evidence on which these dates are based.

4

List of illustrations

1
Introduction

Man and the sea

Two-thirds of the surface of the globe is covered by seas; the remaining third has numerous lakes and rivers, which form both barriers and highways. Until recently these lakes and rivers had imprecise boundaries and in wet seasons considerably extended their basins and channels, whilst coastlines have undergone short and long term changes due to erosion, deposition and variations in sea level. From earliest times man has had both to combat and to make use of these expanses of water to explore and exploit his environment; to extend his settlements and colonise other areas; and to sustain trade and travel in later times.

Almost all significant water barriers were crossed at a remarkably early date. Even at times of much lower sea levels, there were deep channels between western Indonesia and New Guinea, yet archaeological evidence shows that man came to Australia sometime before 40,000 BC, crossing these 80-100 kilometre (50-60 mile) wide channels in his progress from south-east Asia. Mesolithic man of 10,000 BC was able to reach the Mediterranean island of Melos and transport obsidian back to the Greek mainland. Around 7000 BC deep-water catches of fish were being made in the Mediterranean, and further north rising sea levels, which cut off Britain and Ireland from the continent of Europe by the seventh millennium BC, obliged subsequent settlers and traders to use water transport.

There are many examples of the early use of waterborne craft to occupy islands: for example, the colonisation of Melanesia in the south Pacific by 3000 BC, and the subsequent occupation of Micronesia and Polynesia by other groups. But even within land masses water transport would have facilitated man's early expansion, as in his progress from Alaska to the southern tip of South America.

Thus from very early times there is indirect evidence that neither inland waterways nor seas were insurmountable obstacles to man's movements. Well before he had domesticated animals or mastered agricultural and pottery skills he was able to build and use water transport. And from neolithic times onwards he made increasing use of lakes, rivers and the sea as transport routes and as sources of food.

Rafts and boats

I have used the expression 'water transport' above to emphasise that man used rafts as well as boats. Rafts made of logs, reeds or bark have had widespread use on tropical and equatorial seas and on inland waterways in many zones. They differ from boats in that little attempt is made to make them watertight; they float because of the buoyancy of individual elements. Boats, on the other hand, have (almost) watertight hulls which displace water and thereby gain buoyancy. They have been made from logs, bark, reed and skin, in addition to the now ubiquitous plank boat. All these materials are perishable and thus only in special circumstances do ancient rafts and boats survive to be excavated. However, excavated evidence may, in certain times and places, be supplemented by representations of water transport carved on stones or used as decorations on seals and pots, and occasionally small-scale models are found. In addition, written descriptions of the use of rafts and boats survive from some of the early literate civilisations. Study of recent boat types may also help; it is possible to suggest, for example, that because skinboats are in use in the Arctic today similar ones may have been in use there in prehistoric times. Such a line of argument leads to the unexpected possibility that reed rafts may have been used in prehistoric and medieval Europe, for their recent use is known in Ireland, Hungary, Sardinia and Corfu.

In northern and western Europe, the area with which this book principally deals, there is direct evidence only for logboats (dugout canoes), planked boats, skinboats and log rafts in the prehistoric and medieval periods. Other forms of water transport may have been used, but evidence has not survived or has not yet been recognised.

Maritime archaeology

The study of ancient boats and rafts is at the heart of the wider topic, maritime archaeology, which itself merges into the mainstream of the archaeological discipline. Thus the study of how a particular boat was built and what tools were used leads to an investigation of its equipment (anchors, bailers, etc), how it was propelled and steered, how loaded and discharged, and what tasks it was used for (ferrying, fishing, cargo carrying, etc). We then may ask where it was normally used and, if this was at sea, how it was navigated. A related topic is the study of supporting facilities such as landing places (harbours, beacons, leading marks, etc), cargo handling facilities and warehouses, boatbuild-

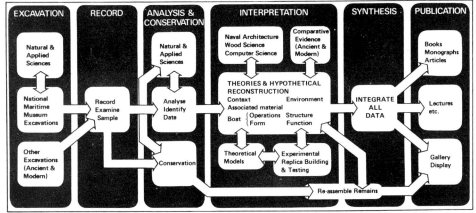

Fig. 1. Flow diagram showing how maritime archaeological research proceeds from excavation to publication.

ing sites, boat houses and slipways, causeways or other approaches to the site from inland. Many of the latter structures are also of direct interest to dry-land archaeologists.

Maritime artifacts and structures may be found underwater (sea or inland), in the inter-tidal zone or on land, and it is not only the remains of buildings that may be found on land, for boats and fish weirs may be found in former watercourses, or on land which was inter-tidal before being enclosed, or on land which has emerged because of relative falls in sea level. In addition, in certain times and places, boats have been used in funeral ceremonies and may be found in grave mounds. Conversely, where there has been a relative rise in sea level, buildings and other structures as well as wrecks may now be found underwater. Thus 'dry' archaeologists and 'wet' archaeologists, and those who are both, are involved in the excavation of maritime artifacts and structures. The area within which they work may be called the maritime zone: this extends to seaward and to landward of the shoreline and includes estuaries, rivers, lakes and the land adjacent to them.

Fig. 1 shows that other specialists are also concerned in this maritime research: botanists, zoologists, geologists and climatologists who are interested in the environment in which the ancient craft were used; scientists carrying out sea level studies; dendrochronologists and radiocarbon dating specialists; naval architects and computer scientists to assess the performance of the boats; historians to study documents which will illuminate

Fig. 2. The early nineteenth-century excavation of a late medieval vessel from a former course of the river Rother, Kent.

maritime activities; art historians to date and possibly interpret representations of boats; placename students to indicate something of the history of the site; and conservators to preserve the remains. Individual archaeologists may be able to undertake some of these additional enquiries — historical research or naval architectural calculations for example — but generally the post-excavation phase of a maritime project is one of teamwork with the archaeologist as co-ordinator.

This book includes material both from Britain and from elsewhere. Boats travel and the bigger ones travel internationally; they may be wrecked far from their home port. They are their own advertisement and a successful design or aspects of it may be copied far from where it originated. In addition, a study of any one country's boat finds would reveal a very incomplete picture of maritime antiquity, so few are the well documented finds. Thus this book deals with northern and western Europe with some comparative material from elsewhere. The time span extends from before the bronze age to the sixteenth century AD.

How the subject developed

Logboat and plank boat remains were found in many places in Europe from the seventeenth century onwards: the logboats were immediately designated 'primitive' and therefore 'prehistoric'; the planked boat remains were said to be 'Viking'. None of the finds were adequately documented and few were preserved. The late medieval vessel found near the river Rother in 1822 is typical of this phase of archaeology. After being excavated (fig. 2), lifted and put on display, it was destroyed when it no longer made a profit.

The modern phase of maritime archaeology may be said to have begun in 1863 with Conrad Engelhardt's excavation of three boats from a bog at Nydam in southern Jutland. One of these survives and is now on display in the museum at Schloss Gottorp, Schleswig (fig. 3). Engelhardt recorded many details of this boat and, although there are doubts about the way the remains have been reassembled (including the addition of modern wood), the remains and the documentation have proved sufficient for later scholars to determine the most likely form of the original fourth-century AD boat.

Towards the end of the nineteenth century and in the early years of the twentieth, further boats were excavated from Viking age burial mounds in Norway (fig. 4). This spectacular group of

Fig. 3. The fourth-century AD Nydam boat on display in Schloss Gottorp, Schleswig. (Copyright: Schleswig-Holstein Landesmuseum.)

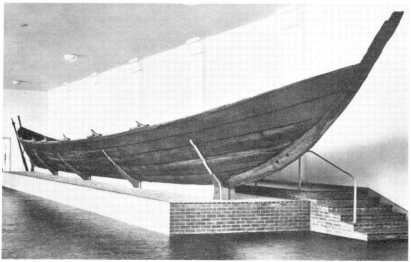

finds fired public interest and stimulated research into Viking age
boatbuilding, the effects of which can be seen today. To explain
these finds Scandinavian scholars drew on medieval documentary
evidence, including the Icelandic sagas, and found analogies for
form and fittings in the contemporary boats of western Norway.
Such was the interest in these Viking ships that a replica of one of
them, the ninth-century Gokstad find, was built and sailed from
Norway to the United States in 1893 (fig. 5).

During this early phase commercial divers, Mediterranean
fishermen and sponge divers occasionally brought to the surface
objects from wreck sites, but the potential that was thus indicated
could not be fully realised until the invention of the aqualung,
self-contained underwater breathing apparatus (SCUBA), by
Cousteau and Gagnan. From *c* 1948 divers with this equipment
were able to work in relative freedom on the seabed, in and
around wreck sites. Archaeologists took up diving and George
Bass set the standard for underwater work in his pioneering
excavation in 1960 of the late bronze age wreck site off Cape
Gelidonya, Turkey.

Archaeology on underwater sites has made much progress
since those early days. The general public may be aware only of
the recovery of spectacular artifacts — amphorae and statues in
the Mediterranean, coins and guns in northern waters — but the
real advance has been in the standard of surveying, recording and
excavating, which is now comparable with that used on land sites.
The differing attitudes to wreck sites of the archaeologist, the
sports diver and the commercial exploiter have at times led to
conflict, and in recent years attempts have been made to regulate
the use of the seabed by these various interests so that there is
minimum loss of archaeologically valuable information. In
Britain underwater wreck sites may be designated as of
archaeological, historic or artistic importance by the Department
of Trade on the advice of a committee representing the interests
of salvors, sports divers, hydrographers, museums and ancient
monuments. Such sites may only be investigated by an authorised
team led by an archaeologist and having access to conservation
facilities. The great majority of sites so far investigated in British
and Irish waters have been of post-medieval ships; in general, on
the few earlier sites only cargo has survived, not ship's structure.
In the Baltic, however, medieval boats have been excavated
underwater, and Classical wrecks have been excavated in the
Mediterranean.

Underwater excavation and salvage work has reached such a

Fig. 4. The early ninth-century AD Oseberg ship during excavation in 1905. (Copyright: Universitetets Oldsaksamling, Oslo.)

Fig. 5. *Viking,* a replica of the ninth-century Gokstad ship, which was sailed from Norway to America in 1893. (Copyright: Norsk Sjofartsmuseum, Oslo.)

Fig. 6. The seventeenth-century royal warship *Wasa* after being raised from the bottom of Stockholm harbour in 1961. (Copyright: SSM Stockholm.)

standard that almost complete ships can be raised: the seventeenth-century wreck of the Swedish royal ship *Wasa* was raised in 1961 (fig. 6); and the remains of the Tudor royal warship *Mary Rose* were recovered from the waters of Spithead in 1982. These are exceptional cases, however, as the costs are tremendous, not least the twenty or so years of conservation which must follow the recovery of the waterlogged hulls. When such resources are not available underwater remains must be recorded on the seabed to such a standard and in such detail that small-scale models could be built or computer drawings compiled. If practicable, important elements of the structure may be lifted so that details can be confirmed. In this way the maximum of information may be retrieved without the heavy costs of salvage, conservation and display of a whole hull.

Scandinavian interest in maritime archaeology was stimulated by the excavation in 1958-62 of five Viking age boats which had formed a blockage at Skuldelev in Roskilde Fjord, Denmark. The initial evaluation and survey was carried out underwater but the excavation by Olsen and Crumlin-Pedersen (fig. 7) was undertaken inside a protective coffer dam which kept out the waters of the fjord. The report on these Skuldelev ships became the model of how to undertake post-excavation work on the remains of a wooden boat — or indeed any wooden structure.

Parallel with the post-war upsurge in archaeology underwater was an increase in the tempo of general archaeology on land caused by drainage schemes as at Kalmar, Sweden, or in the polders of the Netherlands, and by the redevelopment of riverside areas as in London. Research excavations were also undertaken as at the opening of a large burial mound at Sutton Hoo, Suffolk, in 1939, where the impression was revealed of a sixth or seventh century AD boat (fig. 8), some 18 metres (60 feet) long, with spectacular gravegoods. Similar excavations were undertaken at Ladby, Denmark, where the 'ghost' of a Viking age boat was encountered. Less spectacular, but probably of greater significance to maritime archaeology, was the discovery of the remains of three ancient boats on the northern foreshore of the river Humber at North Ferriby, Humberside. In 1937 E. V. Wright and his brother found what they at first assumed was part

Fig. 7. A coffer dam was built around the remains of five Viking age wrecks during excavations in Roskilde Fjord at Skuldelev, Denmark. (Copyright: Ole Crumlin-Pedersen.)

Fig. 8. The 1939 excavation of the impression of a sixth-century AD boat at Sutton Hoo, Suffolk. (Copyright: Barbara Wagstaff.)

of a Viking ship but which subsequently proved to be from the bronze age (fig. 9). The publication of these boats proved to be of great significance to the study of British prehistory as it revolutionised ideas about water transport and woodworking technology and reminded archaeologists that there was a maritime dimension to antiquity several thousand years before the Viking age.

Many archaeologists at some time investigate aspects of maritime antiquity such as trade, migration, sea level changes and waterfront structures. But there is a core to this maritime sub-discipline, the study of water transport, which requires

Fig. 9 *(Left).* One end of the bronze age Ferriby boat 1 protruding from the mud of the Humber foreshore during excavation in 1946.
Fig. 10 *(Right).* The ninth-century AD Graveney boat during excavation from a drainage channel near Whitstable, Kent, in 1970.

specialist knowledge and research techniques. In addition, artifacts recovered from waterlogged sites (whether these be on land or underwater) require special conservation; and boats when recovered need large premises for post-excavation research and subsequent display. Specialist units have therefore been established in the United States, Scandinavia, Germany, the Netherlands, France, Israel, Australia, and at St Andrews, Portsmouth and Greenwich in Britain. The Archaeological Research Centre at the National Maritime Museum, Greenwich, was formed after the chance discovery and rescue excavation of the late ninth-century AD Graveney boat (fig. 10) from a tributary of the river Thames in 1970. Since then the Centre has undertaken much fieldwork, including excavations on land, underwater and in the inter-tidal zone, and has set up a laboratory which specialises in the conservation of waterlogged materials. The information gained about maritime matters between 2000 BC and AD 1500 has been made available in books and lectures and by displays in the museum's Archaeological Gallery (fig. 11).

Fig. 11. A full-scale fibreglass model of the Graveney boat in the Archaeological Gallery at the National Maritime Museum.

2
The maritime archaeologist at work

Excavation

Boat finds, whether excavated archaeologically or found by chance, are seldom complete and are often in a fragmented and degraded state. Their topsides are almost always missing, and the timber recovered is frequently distorted. Exceptions to this general rule are boats and ships which have been used for burials. Although broken and distorted, a great proportion of the burial vessel and its equipment may survive to be excavated as was the case at Oseberg (fig. 4). The Sutton Hoo boat burial is also noteworthy, as in the thirteen centuries between burial and excavation the wood had disintegrated, leaving only an impression in the sandy soil and rows of boat nails. Meticulous excavation by the British Museum revealed this 'ghost' ship (fig. 8), and a great deal was learned about its construction.

The Brigg 'raft' shown in fig. 12 was first exposed in 1888 during excavations for brick clay near the river Ancholme in south Humberside. It was relocated by the National Maritime Museum in 1973 and excavated the following year. Post-excavation research has shown it to have been not a raft but the flat bottom of a plank boat of the seventh or eighth century BC, the sides and ends having not survived.

Brigg, Graveney (fig. 10) and Ferriby (fig. 9) are examples of boat excavations on land: however, in the Mediterranean and the Baltic, and occasionally in British waters, ancient craft are now being excavated underwater. Occasionally it proves possible to remove such a wreck from the water (fig. 6), or to remove the water from the wreck (fig. 7) and then to excavate the wreck using land methods; alternatively the boat may be dismantled and recovered in pieces, as is generally the case on land sites.

Excavation techniques used by maritime archaeologists are standard archaeological ones modified to suit the context of the excavation, be it on land or underwater. Descriptions may readily be found elsewhere: *The North Ferriby Boats* by E. V. Wright; *Sutton Hoo* volume 1, edited by R. L. S. Bruce-Mitford; and *Maritime Archaeology* by K. Muckelroy. In this chapter, therefore, I shall concentrate on the post-excavation phase of research, illustrating the techniques used by reference to recent work in northern and western Europe.

Fig. 12. The late bronze age Brigg 'raft' when first discovered in 1888, near the river Ancholme, South Humberside.

Recording a boat find

By careful examination of the excavated timbers much may be learnt about the parent trees and about the techniques used to turn them into useful members of a boat's structure. The species of wood used for various parts may be identified by microscopic examination of samples; even the form of individual trees may be recognised: for example, long, straight, sound planks indicate a tall forest tree with few knots in its lower length, whereas a curved rib probably came from an isolated, low-branching tree. Counting growth rings and measuring their width will reveal the age of the timber at felling and give some indication of the rate of growth, thereby throwing light on early techniques of woodland management. We may also learn how planking was converted from the log: by splitting the log radially as was generally done for oak; or by fashioning planks in the tangential plane as for pine (fig. 13). The former presence of now missing timbers is indicated by patterns of nail holes or by impressions left in the wood where two timbers were in close contact. Tool marks may also be detected and these may be related to known tool types (fig. 14).

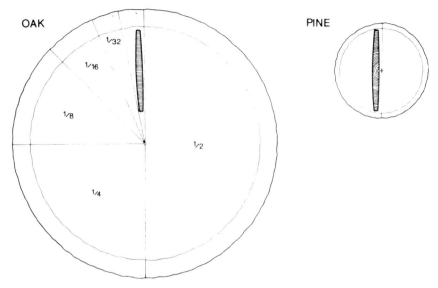

OAK

PINE

1/32
1/16
1/8
1/2
1/4

Fig. 13. The Viking age methods of converting oak and pine logs. (After Crumlin-Pedersen.)
Fig. 14. Viking age woodworking tools from Mastemyr, Sweden. (Copyright: National Museum, Stockholm.)

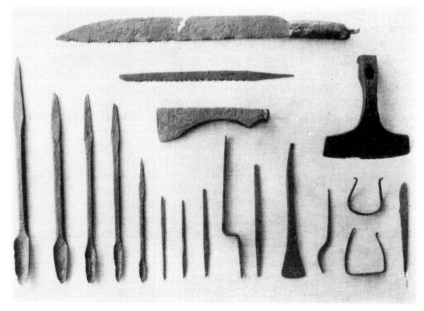

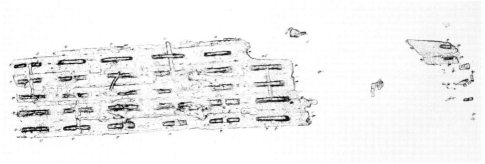

Fig. 15. A stereophotogrammetric contour plot of the Brigg 'raft' during excavation in 1974.

Wear marks may suggest how a boat was rigged or propelled, or they may be an indication of stresses imposed on the structure when underway. Marks on the keel or bottom planking may indicate the use of hard beaches as landing places.

By this sort of detailed examination it is possible not only to deduce something about parts of the boat which have not survived, but also to infer the building sequence and the woodworking techniques used by the builder, and to learn about aspects of the boat's use.

When this examination is completed, or sometimes progressively in step with it, measured drawings are made of individual elements. Generally these drawings are at 1:10 scale, but important features are recorded at full scale and are also photographed. The traditional method of drawing by measured offsets is only one way in which a boat can be recorded: photography, photogrammetry (machine plotting of contours or details seen in three dimensions from a pair of stereo photographs — see fig. 15) and plaster moulds (as at Sutton Hoo and Graveney) have also been used. No single method is the best: they complement one another.

It is also essential to take direct measurements of important features — for example the angle of slope of lengthening joints or scarfs in the planking, the spacing between plank fastenings, and the diameter of nail holes, for even if these appear on scale drawings or photographs precision will be lost if measurements can only be recovered by scaling up.

Interpretation

The excavation and post-excavation records provide the

information upon which hypotheses can be based. The first step in interpretation is to establish the original complete shape of the boat, for only by doing this can we make deductions about the boat's performance — cargo capacity, speed, windward ability and so on. One of the best ways of investigating this is to make a small-scale (say 1:10) model of each element excavated, in cardboard, balsa wood or other light timber. Fastening holes and marks made by adjacent timbers are included, and any post-deposition distortion or shrinkage is allowed for when marking out the shape of these models. An estimate of shrinkage may be made by measuring the differential shrinkage of circular holes — the diameter in the longitudinal plane of the timber remains relatively constant, but diameters in the radial and tangential planes shrink, so that an originally circular hole becomes elliptical (fig. 16). The modelled parts are then assembled by bringing fastening holes into line and placing adjacent timbers on their marked positions: something close to the original form of the incomplete boat should then emerge.

To progress from the known to the unknown, the next stage is to establish the shape of the missing parts of the boat by further model building or by drawings. The reconstructor must remember, however, that there are limits to the flexibility of full-size

Fig. 16. Part of the Brigg 'raft' showing a sewing hole which has shrunk in the tangential direction, thereby becoming elliptical. The triangular shape indicates the longitudinal axis of the parent tree.

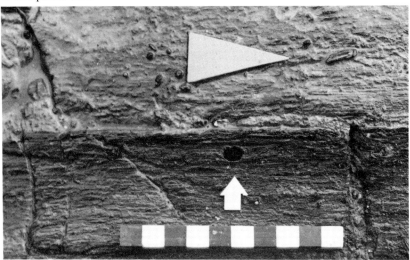

timbers and what is possible on a drawing board or on a 1:10 model may not be practicable on a boatbuilder's bench. It is usually safe to assume that a boat was symmetrical about the fore-and-aft line (although modern examples of non-symmetrical boats are known), and a general symmetry about the midships cross-section may sometimes be postulated. If it can also be assumed that the original boat was seaworthy, stable and useful, then simple naval architectural calculation can help us to reach certain conclusions. As a hypothetical plank or a supporting timber is added to the reconstruction drawing or model, calculations of changes in freeboard, draft and stability will indicate whether seaworthiness and cargo capacity are improved or affected adversely by this element of the reconstruction process. The positioning of fittings can also be checked: if it is thought, for example, that a rudder or an oar pivot should be in a certain position then it must be confirmed that men sitting or standing at the appropriate station could use them.

A study of other excavated boats from the same period and building tradition may also suggest how broken or missing parts of the find should best be theoretically reconstructed. Modern analogies may also help: study of the methods used in twentieth-century small-scale pre-industrial boatbuilding can reveal a range of technical solutions to such general problems as how to close the ends of a boat or how to make one watertight. With caution, the excavated evidence may be re-examined in the light of these possibilities. Such research may also suggest possible uses for timbers of an unusual shape found associated with a boat find but not fastened in position.

Ancient models or representations of boats and ships on pots, coins, town seals or paintings may similarly be a source of ideas for interpreting remains and an aid to the hypothetical reconstruction of their full form. These sources are especially useful for rigging and sails, which very rarely survive. Nevertheless, as with ancient and modern analogies, such evidence must be critically assessed: its compatibility with the excavated remains and with the ancient technological environment must be demonstrated before it can be used with confidence as an aid to reconstruction.

In general there will be more than one solution to the problem of theoretically reconstructing the original form of an incomplete boat find. Where only the bottom of a boat is excavated, several forms of topsides may be compatible with it. If part of the sides also survives then this range of possibilities is reduced; nevertheless several reconstructions can still be compatible with the

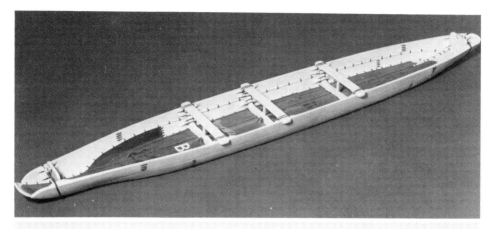

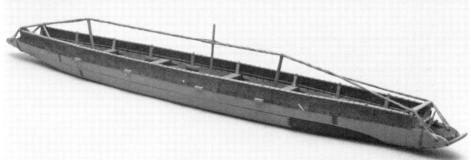

Fig. 17 *(Top).* The minimum solution — two-strake — reconstruction model of Ferriby boat 1. The dark parts represent excavated material; the remainder is conjectural.
Fig. 18 *(Above).* Another 1:10 reconstruction model of Ferriby boat 1, with three strakes (the top one of skin) and a conjectural hogging truss.

excavated remains, as can be seen for example in the Ferriby boat display in the National Maritime Museum (figs. 17 and 18). Such reconstruction models and drawings of variant solutions are hypotheses, not to be confused with the original. They may be close to the original form but new evidence may emerge when the boat timbers are reassembled after conservation or from future excavations of similar boats, and improved research techniques may one day show that aspects of the reconstructions are wrong: in any of these cases the drawings and models will have to be revised.

From these hypothetical reconstructions deductions may be made about the time taken to build such a boat, the size of crew required and how much cargo could be carried. Estimates may also be made of speed, stability and seaworthiness in different sea states, possibly using computer-aided simulation studies. Certain parameters must be fixed, however, before this can be undertaken: we must, for example, establish the density of likely loads, and the height and weight of crew, passengers and live cargo such as cattle may also be significant in stability calculations. In addition, operational data need to be estimated: the size and shape of the water-plane area of a boat markedly influences stability, and to establish the waterline we must decide what would have been a reasonable compromise between draft and freeboard to the ancient seaman. Similarly, estimates must be made of how much bilge water would be tolerated, as a freely moving body of water within a boat may make it unstable.

It can be seen therefore that precise statements about performance can seldom be made: rather, a range of values is given, reflecting the variability in the different assumptions made, the parameters adopted, and the several hypothetical reconstructions postulated. There is a further variability which probably can never be allowed for: different seamen in comparable conditions obtain better or worse performances out of the same boat.

Experimental archaeology

In certain circumstances it is possible to test hypothetical reconstructions by building a full-size replica and carrying out trials. The process of building a replica may eliminate some of the theoretical solutions to details of the design, as their impracticability becomes apparent. In addition, the replica can be evaluated in various sea and wind conditions, under different forms of propulsion and carrying different cargoes, and comparisons made with the theoretical calculations of performance. The effects of varying different parameters or of using, say, different types of rudder may also be investigated, and it may prove possible to determine how close to the wind the original craft might have sailed. Data from such experiments may be of great value in setting up comprehensive theoretical models for analysis by computer.

In 1972-3 the National Maritime Museum built a replica of the smallest of the three boats found inside the Gokstad ship in its Viking age burial mound. The reassembled remains of this

Fig. 19. The ninth-century AD *faering,* or four-oared boat, from Gokstad on display at Bigdoy near Oslo. (Copyright: Universitetets Oldsaksamling, Oslo.)

ninth-century four-oared boat, or *faering,* are now in the Viking Ship Hall near Oslo (fig. 19), and it was decided to build a replica of it as it now is, rather than attempt to determine the validity of the reconstruction work done on the remains in the 1930s. The aims of this Greenwich experiment were to learn about Viking age boatbuilding and seamanship and to gain experience so that authentic replicas might be built of future boat finds.

The 6.51 metre (21 foot) replica was built by Harold Kimber, a master boatbuilder from Somerset, using drawings prepared by Arne Emil Christensen of the Universitetets Oldsaksamling, Oslo (figs. 20 and 21), and sea trials were undertaken in the tidal reaches of the river Tamar at Plymouth (fig. 22). The replica proved to be a fine boat, more stable than it might appear from its lines. Its performance was assessed as objectively as possible with different rowing and steering configurations, with varying loads, and in a range of weather conditions.

What was learnt from this experiment? We learnt about Viking age boatbuilding methods; we learnt how to handle a boat of this type using Viking pattern oars; and we learnt much about the

Fig. 20. The Greenwich *faering* replica during building. The stem has been scarfed to the keel and two strakes have been fastened in position each side.

Fig. 21. The Greenwich *faering*. After the shell of keel, stems and planking has been built, a transverse floor timber or rib has been placed in position. The other timbers are temporary ones to stabilise the form of the boat until further ribs are fastened.

Fig. 22. The Greenwich *faering* under oars during trials in Plymouth Sound.

Fig. 24 *(Above).* The boss on which the *faering* replica's side rudder pivots.

Fig. 23 *(Left).* The bows of the Greenwich replica showing the forward inclined frame or bulkhead with two holes piercing it.

achievements and difficulties of archaeological experiments. Fig.
23 illustrates in one small way what may be gained by such
practical trials. Working from the 1:10 drawings, we made holes
in the forward bulkhead of the replica of the required size and
shape. When we came to use the boat, it became natural to seek
handholds to haul it out of the water, and this is what these holes
were probably for, but we had made them too small when scaling
up from the drawings. The *faering's* side rudder pivots about an
external boss (fig. 24), and sea trials showed how critical was the
balance of rudder on boss. Had we got the exact shape of the
original boss and had we dished the rudder sufficiently so that it
fitted snugly against it? If not, then we were not testing a true
replica of the original steering system, and in this respect the
performance of our twentieth-century replica could not be said to
be that of the ninth-century boat.

Considerations such as these helped us to formulate principles
for boatbuilding experiments. In summary, these require that
authenticity should be paramount in the choice of boat to be
copied, place to build, and construction methods and tools to use,
departure from authenticity being permitted only when this has a
small, measurable effect and only when a rigorous argument for
doing so can be stated. Experimental work requires as much
planning as an excavation, and it is essential that a full written and
photographic record be kept so that the authenticity of the replica
and the value of the experiment can be assessed by others.

Conservation and display

If the excavated boat remains have been considered of
sufficient importance to warrant recovery, then they will become
important primary evidence. It is thus essential that they are
conserved by a method which maintains their excavated form and
dimensions as closely as possible. Recently deposited timbers
which are not fully waterlogged and are therefore only slightly
degraded may be stabilised by allowing them to dry slowly, but
more degraded timbers, which could not support their own
weight if dried, require some form of active conservation.

One treatment that has generally proved successful is the use of
polyethylene glycol (PEG), a wax which is soluble in water. The
waterlogged timber is immersed in warm water with a low
concentration of PEG; as this concentration is increased by daily
additions of PEG, the liquid wax replaces the water in the
degraded wood. When a concentration exceeding seventy per

Fig. 25. The Oseberg ship on display at Bigdoy near Oslo. Compare with fig. 4. New wood has replaced degraded or missing timbers.

cent is reached the timber is removed from the solution and the wax sets into solid form, supporting the internal structure of the wood. There may be some shrinkage from excavated dimensions, of the order of two per cent radial and four per cent tangential: shrinkage greater than this would make it difficult to reassemble the timbers in a coherent manner. A variant of this tank treatment is to spray the timber with PEG solution: this may be used for large ship finds which cannot be dismantled. The PEG tank process takes many months for individual pieces of wood, and therefore a boat find can take two to three years to conserve, depending on the tank capacity available. Spraying is slower; it has, for example, taken over twenty years to complete the conservation of the *Wasa* by this method. Other methods of conserving waterlogged wood are known but none has yet proved as effective as PEG for large timbers.

Figs. 25 and 26 show two methods of displaying reassembled boat remains. In Oslo new wood was added to complete the full shape of the Oseberg ship, whereas in the Roskilde display of the

Fig. 26. Skuldelev ship 1 on display at Roskilde, Denmark. Only excavated wood is displayed. (Copyright: Ole Crumlin-Pedersen.)

Fig. 27. A 1:10 scale model of the Graveney boat: the dark parts represent excavated material.

Skuldelev boats only original wood is displayed (except where an obviously plastic replica is used instead of timber still under conservation) and the deduced full shape is seen in tubular framework. These methods each show only one solution to the reconstruction problem. An alternative is to display the remains (or replicas of them) without added reconstruction, so that a visitor may visualise his own solution, and to present several possible reconstructions nearby. This has been done at the National Maritime Museum, where small models and drawings of alternative reconstructions are placed alongside full-scale displays showing the Graveney and Ferriby boats as found (figs. 17, 18 and 27).

Publication

The information about a boat find obtained from the recording, model building, experimental and reassembly stages of research has to be integrated to form a coherent whole. To this is added knowledge gained from artifacts found with or near the boat. Dating evidence must be evaluated: the circumstances of the find may mean that no datable artifacts are found and the stratigraphy is difficult to interpret. However, wooden boats readily lend themselves to dating by radiocarbon analysis, and dendrochronological dating may be available for medieval oak timbers. Analysis of the buried surface under the boat and the identification of pollen and of other floral and faunal remains can enable a picture to be built up of the environment in which the boat was lost or abandoned.

As fig. 1 shows, the end of an archaeological investigation is the publication of a synthesis of all the evidence by book, lecture or display. In this way knowledge of the find is disseminated, and interpretations and deductions become subject to criticism and evaluation. In a sense, a project is never finished: publication stimulates other projects, theoretical and practical, and thus progress is made.

3

Water transport in northern and western Europe

Of the theoretical range of nine basic forms of water transport, only four (log rafts, skinboats, logboats and plank boats) appear in the archaeological record. Two other forms are globally rare (reed boats, found only in Arabia, and bark bundle rafts, formerly used in Tasmania); and buoyed rafts are traditionally associated with lower latitudes. It might be expected, however, that reed rafts and bark boats were used in ancient Europe, but direct evidence for them has not been recognised, if it has survived.

Logboat remains are probably the most numerous, but the majority of them are inadequately reported and very few are dated. An increasing number of plank boats are reasonably well documented and dated, but these finds are unevenly spread over northern and western Europe and come from a period of over three thousand years. Even with a generous assessment of the quantity of the remains, the quality of the report and the accuracy of the dating, there are only five plank boat finds from the prehistoric period, fifteen from Roman times, six from the fifth to seventh centuries AD, fifty from the eighth to twelfth centuries and twenty from the thirteenth to fifteenth centuries. Many of these are mere fragments and contribute little to our general knowledge. However, there is some clustering of finds where several boats from a region are roughly of the same date: the river Humber in the prehistoric period; the river Rhine during Roman times; Viking age Scandinavian; and the region between the Rhine and the Baltic in the later middle ages. Only from these groups can useful generalisations be made and thus, rather than a continuous history of water transport in northern and western Europe, we get blocks of information, valid for certain regions and limited periods of time, with only slight indications of what happened at other times and places. Documentary and icono-graphic evidence allows us to fill out this picture presented by archaeology but there are still great gaps in our knowledge of boat and ship building.

Names of ship and boat types are recorded in medieval documents but by no means all boat finds can be allocated to such

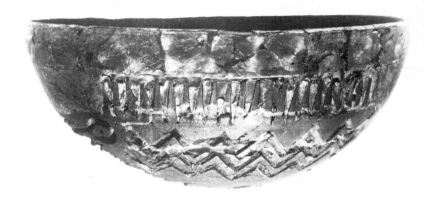

Fig. 28. The bowl of shale from Caergwrle, Clwyd, which may be a representation of a skinboat. (Copyright: National Museum of Wales.)

a type. Even more rarely can the name of a find be established. Most finds from before *c* 1500 are anonymous, being now identified by a site name and sequential number: Sutton Hoo 2, Ferriby 3 and so on. An exception is a wreck in the river Hamble near Bursledon which, from documentary and dating evidence, seems almost certainly to be Henry V's *Grace Dieu*.

A theoretical study of man's technological abilities as evidenced by tools and worked material indicates that during the upper palaeolithic (say 40,000 to 8000 BC) he was technically capable of building rafts of reed, bark or logs, and skinboats of a simple construction. By neolithic times (say 4000 BC) all the basic types of water transport, including simple plank boats, could theoretically have been built. There are, however, no finds from these periods to confirm such speculations, except for some logboats dated to the late neolithic and a possible one from the seventh millennium BC. Caesar described how the Celts used log rafts to cross the river Rhine and two rafts dated to the second century AD have been excavated at Strasbourg; otherwise there is little information about rafts in northern and western Europe until the post-medieval period. The main evidence of water transport is thus for logboats and plank boats from the bronze age onwards,with limited evidence for skinboats.

Skinboats

There is some evidence for skinboats during the bronze age but it is neither plentiful nor strong. Rock carvings in Scandinavia and northern Russia have been interpreted as representations of them but such carvings are difficult to interpret and date. The small model, made of shale, from Caergwrle, Clwyd (fig. 28), which is generally dated to this period, has also been taken to represent a skinboat, but this is by no means certain.

Not until Roman times is there significant evidence. Caesar, Pliny and other authors describe the use of skinboats in Italy, Spain and Britain, and the *Massaliote Periplus*, an early form of pilotage handbook, indicates that sea-going versions were used for voyages between Brittany, Britain and Ireland. A 180 millimetre (7 inch) gold model from Broighter, near Limavady in County Derry may represent this form of boat (see the cover photograph). This model, which was part of a hoard discovered in the mid nineteenth century and dated to the first century BC, had nine pairs of oars, and a mast and yard show that sail was also used; steering was by an oar over the quarter. Also with the model were boat hooks, and poles which may have been for punting.

Skin and the insubstantial timbers used for the framework of a currach or coracle survive much less well than the timber of a logboat or plank boat. Skinboat remains are therefore almost unknown, but traces are thought to have been found of ones used for burials during the Roman period in south Humberside and in the early bronze age at Dalgety, Fife, Scotland. These remains were vestigial and neither report adds to our knowledge of skinboat construction. A timber from the tenth-century site at Ballinderry, County Westmeath, however, seems to be a longitudinal member of a skinboat frame.

The use of skinboats in and around Britain and Ireland is sporadically documented from the fifth century onwards, and later medieval skinboat builders are known to have tanned cattle hides in oak bark and fastened them to a frame of open wickerwork. Other evidence comes from a boat identified as a currach carved on the eighth-century stone cross shaft at Bantry in County Cork, which seems to be propelled by six oarsmen, each with a single oar. Using this sort of information and a knowledge of boatbuilding methods used in the west of Ireland, Timothy Severin built an 11 metre (36 foot) skinboat (fig. 29) and in 1976-7 sailed her across the Atlantic via Iceland. Although relatively slow, she proved to have considerable stability, remaining fairly dry in rough Atlantic seas. In fair weather with two square sails she could make 30 to 60 miles (50-100 km) a day,

Fig. 29. The skinboat *Brendan* in which Tim Severin and his crew crossed the Atlantic in 1976-7. (Copyright: Tim Severin.)

but she made considerable leeway (drift downwind) when attempting to tack to windward.This experiment has given us a general idea of the performance of a sea-going skinboat.

Logboats

A number of logboats, dated to the bronze age by radiocarbon assay, have been found in several European countries. The oldest one from Britain is that from Locharbriggs, Dumfriesshire, of *c* 2000 BC. Three other logboats from south Humberside (Appleby, Short Ferry and Brigg) are from the ninth to eleventh centuries BC. The Brigg logboat (fig. 30) had been made from an oak tree which must have been at least 15 metres (49 feet) in length, with a diameter at the lower end of about 1.9 metres (6.2 feet), that is a circumference of almost 6 metres (19.5 feet). In hollowing out this log ninety per cent of the wood was worked away to produce a boat 14.78 metres long (48 feet) with a bottom thickness of about 100 millimetres (4 inches) and sides of about 50 millimetres (2 inches). The bow end was rounded; the stern, however, was open where the log had been hollowed right through (probably because this lower end of the log had been infected by heart rot) and was subsequently made watertight by a vertical transom board fitted into a groove and caulked with moss. A theoretical analysis of this logboat shows that it could have carried a crew of twenty-eight men in only 380 millimetres (15 inches) of water. It would certainly have been an impressive sight and could have achieved comparatively good speed when propelled by a full crew but was probably difficult to manoeuvre in a confined space; such considerations may indicate a prestige rather than a practical role. The other British logboats from this period are also of oak: they are smaller than Brigg and thus probably more useful as ferries or for fishing, fowling and the transport of reeds and other materials.

A number of logboats have been dated to the iron age, and Roman authors mention their use in Spain, France and Germany. Two logboats from the river Rhine at Zwammerdam, Netherlands, have their midship section pierced with holes to form a free-flooding fish well between watertight bulkheads. A logboat

Fig. 30. The Brigg logboat in 1886. It was lost when Hull Museum burned down in 1944.

Fig. 31. The bow of the iron age Poole logboat with an imitation stem carved in the solid log. (Copyright: Poole Museums.)

from Poole Harbour, Dorset, dated to the third or fourth century BC, has the underside of the bow fashioned into the shape of a stem (fig. 31), indicating that its builders were familiar with plank boats having true stems. This logboat, which is being conserved in the museum buildings at Poole, was made from half of an oak log that had been split longitudinally, unlike the earlier Brigg logboat, which was made from a whole log. The 11 metre (36 foot) Poole boat had very good capacity, being able to carry 1,723 kilograms (3,800 pounds) of cargo and four men in less than 400 millimetres (16 inches) of water, or eighteen men in less than 300 millimetres (1 foot) of water. Because of its low density a load of turf (peat) will have a higher centre of gravity than the equivalent weight of stone and thus its potential for making a boat unstable is greater. This Poole boat would have remained stable with a maximum load of turf, whereas the Brigg logboat would only be stable with a heavy load such as stone or men kneeling. Comparisons of performance such as these may be made when sufficient remains are found to enable valid reconstructions of the original boats to be made.

Thirty out of the fifty European logboats so far dated are later than the first century AD: thus not all logboats are prehistoric, as was assumed until recently. The latest logboat surviving in Britain is that from Giggleswick Tarn, North Yorkshire (fig. 32), dated to the mid fourteenth century. This 2.45 metre (8 foot) logboat is unique in Britain, having been made from an ash log rather than oak. Specially shaped timbers had been fitted across the ends to prevent the log from splitting, as evidently happened to others. The stern fitting could also be used as a seat by the paddler (fig. 33); the bow timber was dovetail-shaped at the ends and fitted into a correspondingly shaped groove. Along the sides long, thin timbers had been fastened to strengthen the boat longitudinally and possibly to give it extra stability when used at deep drafts. This medieval boat was used on the lake at Giggleswick and possibly on the river Ribble to carry some form of heavy cargo. Thus, at a time when great ships were being built in the ports of southern Britain, a modest logboat was still of use to a local community in the highland zone. There is documentary evidence for the use of logboats in Ireland and Scotland in the seventeenth and eighteenth centuries, and in Scandinavia and Germany they were in use in the early twentieth century.

By the time the Giggleswick boat was first recorded in 1976 it had shrunk, and this is true of almost every logboat to be seen in

Fig. 32. The fourteenth-century AD ash logboat from Giggleswick Tarn, North Yorkshire, after being reassembled at the National Maritime Museum. The detached timbers formerly fitted outboard along the top of the sides.

Fig. 33. A 1:10 scale model of the Giggleswick boat with model crewman sitting on the stern.

museums today. Unless an active conservation method is used, waterlogged wood shrinks markedly as it dries out. In some cases this will cause the boat to fragment, but even when the log remains more or less a single unit it will shrink in breadth and in height of sides (the longitudinal shrinkage being in general insignificant). Thus many logboats were originally some twenty per cent greater in breadth and height than they appear today in museums. The majority of measurable logboats from southern Britain were originally between 2.77 and 4.65 metres (9-15 feet) in length and 730 to 990 millimetres (28 to 39 inches) in breadth; they are now roughly the same length but their breadths have shrunk to 600 to 820 millimetres (24 to 32 inches).

It sometimes proves possible to identify a local tradition of boatbuilding as, for example, in north-west England, where, between 1889 and 1971, fragments of eleven logboats were found on a 3 mile (5 km) stretch of the river Mersey near Warrington, and two others from riverine sites some 8 miles (13 km) north-east towards Manchester. Eight of these boats have radiocarbon dates which indicate that they were probably in use during the twelfth century AD. Although there is some variation, these boats have sufficient characteristics in common to suggest that they conformed to a local tradition in logboat building: they were made from tapering oak logs some 4 metres (13 feet) in length and had rounded ends and cross-sections; transverse timbers were fastened across the ends by trenails 25 millimetres (1 inch) in diameter; and ridges were left across the bottom near the ends, probably for the paddler to push his feet against.

A 4.3 metre (14 foot) oak rowing boat (fig.34) excavated from the former lake at Kentmere, Cumbria, by Dr David Wilson and now in the National Maritime Museum, seems to have originally been a logboat whose rotten or damaged sides were replaced by clinker-laid planking supported by four birch ribs. It thus became a logboat extended by planking, a concept which has been postulated as the prehistoric origin of the fully planked boat. However, this Kentmere find has been dated to *c* AD 1300, a

Fig. 34. The planked boat from Kentmere, Cumbria, of *c* AD 1300, during excavation in 1955.

salutary reminder that dating boats solely by typological considerations is not yet practicable: radiocarbon dating remains the
one reliable method for boats found without datable artifacts and
not in a datable context.

Plank boats: bronze age

Four planked boats have survived from the bronze age: the
three boats from North Ferriby (fig. 9) dated to the middle of the
second millennium BC, and the so-called 'raft' from Brigg of
700-800 BC (figs. 12 and 15). All four boats were built of oak
planks sewn together with bindings of withies, yew at Ferriby and
willow at Brigg. The seams between the planks were made
watertight by a caulking of moss held in place by a fore-and-aft
lath under the stitching. The bottom planks of these boats were
further linked together by timbers aligned across them and
passing through holes in cleats which projected vertically from
the upper surface of the planking (figs. 9 and 12). All four boats
show a high standard of woodworking craftsmanship.

Two reconstruction models of Ferriby boat 1 are shown in figs.
17 and 18; both are based on the excavated evidence but the one
in fig. 18 has had a third strake of skin rather than wood added to
give it higher sides without a great increase in topweight. This
version could therefore carry more load or have greater
freeboard (vertical distance between the waterline and the top of
the sides) than the minimum solution model of two strakes (fig.
17). The three-strake model has also been fitted with a simple
hogging truss or rope from bow to stern to increase its
longitudinal strength and give it the ability to be operated in
rougher sea conditions. It has been calculated that a 15 metre (51
foot) boat based on the simple model could have carried a load of
3 tonnes (crew and cargo) with a draft of only 300 millimetres (12
inches) and a freeboard of 360 millimetres (14 inches). If the
freeboard could be reduced to 260 millimetres (10 inches), which
would probably be safe in fair weather, 5.5 tonnes could be
carried with a draft of 400 millimetres (16 inches).

Ferriby boat 1 and the Brigg 'raft' are long and relatively
narrow but, whereas the former becomes narrower towards the
ends and thus has a recognisable 'boat' form, the 'raft', when
reconstructed,is not unlike an open, rectangular box measuring
some 12.30 by 2.32 metres (40 by 7.6 feet). The vertical sides and
ends may have consisted of two strakes, when the height would
have been only 340 millimetres (13 inches), or three strakes,
bringing the height to 550 millimetres (22 inches). This was a

flat-bottomed boat — not a raft — of a form still used on some inland waterways and in inshore waters. It was probably used as a ferry to cross the tidal Ancholme near Brigg, where the valley narrows. With a side height of 340 millimetres (13 inches) this boat could have safely carried about 2.58 tonnes (say forty sheep and ten men) with a draft of about 250 millimetres (10 inches); with sides of 550 millimetres (22 inches) a load of 8.10 tonnes (say thirty cattle and ten men) would have been possible with a draft of about 380 millimetres (15 inches). The 'raft', like the Ferriby boats, was propelled by paddles or possibly by poles (punted in the shallows).

Plank boats: iron age and the Roman period

The remains of a round-bottom, sewn-plank boat were found in the early twentieth century at Hjortspring on the island of Als, Denmark, and dated by association to *c* 350-300 BC. The boat was of limewood with two strakes each side fastened together by lime bast cord, and the sewing holes were filled with resin. The planking overlapped at the edges, but with smooth outer and inner faces: this technique appears to be a forerunner of the clinker method of fastening planks used in the Viking age and in recent times. It is estimated that the Hjortspring boat was 13-14 metres (43-46 feet) long with a 2 metre (6.6 foot) beam; it was propelled by paddles. A replica of this craft was built in Denmark in 1971 but as lime of the original dimensions could not be obtained the replica was less deep and much less broad and thus did not have the stability or the capacity of the original boat.

Caesar and Strabo tell us something about the boats used by the Celtic Veneti in the first century BC off the coast of north-west France. These flat-bottomed boats with high bow and stern had thick oak planking caulked with moss, leather sails, and anchors with chains. They were obviously better suited to the local conditions than the Roman vessels for they could more readily enter shallows and take the ground. The boats of the Veneti seem to have been more in the Ferriby/Brigg tradition than that of Hjortspring.

A group of boats found near the river Rhine in the Nether-lands, Belgium, France and Switzerland seem to have been typical of the boats used by the Celts on inland waterways during the first to third centuries AD (fig. 35). There is variation in the building methods used, but generally these craft were of barge-like shape, long and narrow with flat bottoms, low vertical sides and slightly rising ends. A distinctive feature was that the

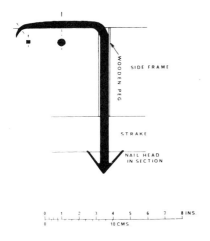

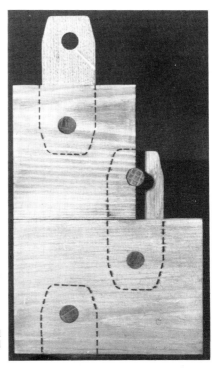

Fig. 36 *(Above)*. Method of fastening the strakes of Romano-Celtic boats to the side frames or ribs by driving a nail through a trenail or wooden peg and then turning the point of the nail back into the rib. (After Peter Marsden.)

Fig. 37 *(Right)*. Model showing the method of fastening the planking of Roman and other classical ships.

planking was not fastened together; but the ribs (floor timbers) were fastened to the planking by iron nails which were clenched by turning the tip backwards into the timber on the inside of the boat (fig. 36). A second century AD sea-going vessel excavated from the river Thames at Blackfriars, London, also had these and other characteristic 'Romano-Celtic' features.

Two or three finds in north-west Europe (one of them the third or fourth century AD County Hall wreck excavated from the south bank of the river Thames in London in 1910) have features linking them to Roman wrecks known from the Mediterranean. The planking in these craft is fastened edge to edge by the insertion of loose tenons into mortices cut at intervals in opposing edges within the thickness of each plank. These tenons were then held in position by trenails (dowels) driven through them at right angles (fig. 37). Although the County Hall wreck was recovered, little now remains of it.

Fig. 35 *(Opposite)*. Zwammerdam boat 6, a flat-bottomed 'barge' of about the second century AD from the lower Rhine. (Copyright: University of Amsterdam.)

Plank boats in the Viking tradition

From the late fourth century AD onwards there are a number of finds from Scandinavia and Britain linked by similarities of form, structure, propulsion and steering. The classic phase of this building tradition occurred during the Viking age (*c* AD 800 to 1100), but ships of this general type were still being used as late as the fifteenth century. The Nydam boat of *c* AD 400 and now on display in the Schloss Gottorp Museum, Schleswig (fig. 3), was a *c* 24 metre (79 foot) rowing boat with thin clinker planking fastened by clenched nails. The central bottom member of the hull was a keel-plank (broader than deep), rather than a true keel (deeper than broad), and the boat had stems at both ends, making it almost symmetrical about its midships section. The ribs (floor timbers) were worked from crooks (tree limbs chosen because they had the appropriate curve) and were fastened to the hull symmetrically about the keel-plank, *after* the planking had been finished. It was propelled by fifteen oars each side, worked in grommets against wooden pivots (tholes) projecting above the top strake of planking, and was steered by a side rudder. Sutton Hoo 2, which survived only as an impression in the sand of an early seventh-century royal burial mound in East Anglia (fig. 8), was generally of the same form and construction. Differences in detail between these two boats include: Sutton Hoo's oar pivots (tholes) were nailed to the top strake rather than lashed; its ribs were trenailed rather than lashed; it had more planks per strake; and the longitudinal curve of the upper edge of the hull (the sheer) was increased. These two boats and fragments of others from Scandinavia may be thought of as forerunners of the Viking age ships.

From the period AD 800 to 1100 there are about thirty boat finds which help to build up a picture of the typical ship or boat built in the heyday of this Viking tradition. The characteristics of pre-Viking age boats were perfected by Viking age shipbuilders. One apparent change is the introduction of the mast, for which there is evidence on Viking age remains; but sailing must have been prevalent in northern Europe well before this time, for mast and sail can be seen on ships carved on sixth-century memorial stones in Gotland. The essential features of Viking age shipbuilding can be seen on figs. 19, 25, 26, 38 and 39. Within this tradition craft were built for different functions: cargo ships, broad and deep-sided in proportion to their length, with a hold amidships and rowing positions only near the bow and stern; warships with a full complement of rowing positions and long in proportion to

Fig. 38 *(Above).* Reconstruction model of Viking age inshore cargo boat Skuldelev 3.

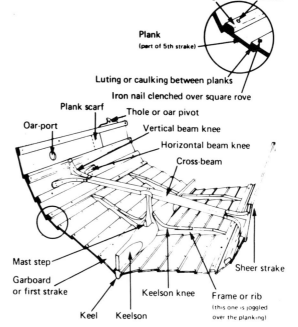

Fig. 39 *(Right).* Features of the Viking boatbuilding tradition.

their breadth; and smaller boats with many of the longship's features, but used as ferries or for fishing. During this period of three hundred years or so there were developments in building practices, such as different methods of fastening the ribs to the planking and variations in the number and position of cross-beams, but these changes are difficult to date precisely — further research and future finds may clarify this and also tell us more about the sail and rigging, for which there is little direct evidence.

Ships and boats built in the eastern Baltic at this time had many of the characteristics described above but two important differences have been identified in some of them: the mast in the eastern craft was generally stepped in a transverse timber rather than in the longitudinal timber (keelson) positioned on top of the keel of the Scandinavian ship; and the clinker planking was fastened by trenails rather than iron nails, with a caulking of moss rather than hair or wool. The full range of similarities and differences between these two variants has not yet been established: further research is required.

Since the 1960s several replicas of Viking craft have been built in Scandinavia but the authenticity of their construction has seldom been demonstrated and many have not been fully published so that valid conclusions cannot yet be drawn about the performance of Viking age craft. A replica of one of the small boats found inside the ninth-century Gokstad royal burial ship, which was built by the National Maritime Museum during 1972-3 (figs. 19-24), achieved an unexpectedly high speed of 7 knots under oars. Theory indicates that such long, light displacement craft should indeed have high speed potential: it is probable that they achieve this by riding up in the water into a semi-planing attitude in favourable conditions under oar or sail. Relatively deep keels and the characteristic steepness of the lower strakes imply that Viking hulls probably had a relatively good windward performance; but how close they could get to the wind is a matter for speculation — possibly not closer than six points, that is about 70 degrees off the wind.

Post-Viking age ships of this tradition have only rarely been excavated but there are representations of them on Irish monuments and on English, Irish and French town seals of the thirteenth and fourteenth centuries (fig. 40). The rigging becomes more complex, castles are added forward and aft, and crossbeams protrude through the sides. A ship type *ceol* or keel is mentioned in English documents at around this time and it seems possible that it refers to ships built generally in the Viking tradition.

Fig. 40. The early fourteenth-century AD seal of Winchelsea, East Sussex, depicting a ship of the post-classic phase of the Viking tradition.

The Graveney boat

The Graveney boat of the late ninth century (figs. 10 and 11) has some features in common with contemporary Viking ships but is different in other aspects and thus, at best, can only be at the margin of this tradition. The bottom and two-thirds of the length of this 14 metre (46 foot) boat were excavated from a tributary of the Thames in 1970 and the remains are now being conserved at the National Maritime Museum. It was clinker-built like a Viking ship but, unlike that type, had heavy, closely spaced floor timbers, probably so that it could carry a dense cargo such as stone. Rather than a graceful continuous curve from keel to stems, as in the Viking tradition, the Graveney boat's stem has a pronounced angle at its lower end, reminiscent of a cog (see below). Thus there are suggestions in this boat's construction of influence from several traditions; alternatively it may represent an as yet undefined tradition, further evidence of which has yet to be excavated or recognised.

There is evidence that the Graveney boat was originally propelled by a sail and converted to a lighter or barge in later years. Theoretical calculations indicate that it would have had good stability, although it might have shipped water amidships in a beam sea. With four or five men manning rowing sweeps (large oars) it could have made about 3 knots, or under sail in suitable winds, 5 to 7 knots. It was capable of sea voyages carrying a cargo of 6 or 7 tonnes.

The cog tradition
During the early middle ages the Frisians of the Rhine estuary and islands established themselves as important seafarers: they played a prominent part in Anglo-Saxon maritime affairs for example and traded with the Baltic. A type of craft known as a *cog* is mentioned in ninth-century and later documents and was evidently prominent in this Frisian trade. Coins from ninth-century Haithabu (Hedeby) on the Baltic coast of Germany depict a flat-bottomed craft with a distinctive angular transition to the stems, rather than the rounded transition of contemporary craft in the Viking tradition.

In the 1950s Fliedner established a link between this type name *cog* and ships depicted on town seals of the thirteenth and fourteenth centuries, with clinker side planking and a single mast and squaresail (fig.41). It thus seems possible that the ninth-century Hedeby representations were also cogs.

Certain changes in cog design may be noted on these thirteenth and fourteenth century town seals: the stern rudder replaced the side rudder in about 1245, for example, and the false stem was introduced around 1280. The most important source of knowledge about this late stage of the cog-building tradition comes, however, from a 23.50 metre (77 foot) wreck found in 1962 during dredging operations in the river Weser near Bremen. It had the characteristic flat bottom and clinker sides with the angular transitions from bottom to stems (fig. 42), and it was dated by dendrochronology to *c* 1380. This Bremen cog is now reassembled and undergoing conservation, but already important

Fig. 41. The town seal of Stralsund, Germany, of *c* AD 1329, showing a vessel in the late cog tradition.

and possibly diagnostic features are known: the plank-fastening iron nails are clenched by turning the tip back into the timber (not unlike the technique used to fasten planking to ribs in the Romano-Celtic boats of the second and third centuries AD); and the caulking of moss is kept in place in the seams by laths and butterfly-shaped iron clamps.

A number of other wrecks dated from the thirteenth to early sixteenth centuries, from Poland, Sweden, Denmark and the Netherlands, have some, but not all, of the characteristics which are at present thought to define this cog tradition. As more flat-bottomed finds are recorded the essential diagnostic features of a cog will emerge and changes over time and regional variations will be recognised. Boats evidently of this general tradition continued to be used to the end of the medieval period,

Fig. 42. The Bremen cog of *c* AD 1380 being reassembled in the Deutches Schiffahrts-museum, Bremerhaven. (Copyright: DSM.)

Fig. 43. The late eighth or early ninth century AD Utrecht boat 1 on display in the Centraal Museum, Utrecht, Netherlands.

but sea-going ships, like the Bremen cog, were also built. Indeed, documents of the thirteenth and fourteenth centuries indicate that during this period the cog succeeded the ship of the Viking tradition as the dominant sea-going type.

The 'hulc' tradition

Boats depicted on coins minted by Charlemagne (late eighth to early ninth century) in the Frisian town of Dorestad on the Rhine show a vessel, banana-shaped in outline, with the side planking running in a similar curve to end well above the waterline; a side rudder is in use and possibly oars as well as a sail. An 18 metre (59 foot) boat found at Utrecht in 1930 generally resembles these Dorestad boats in outline shape and in having a side rudder. The Utrecht boat (fig. 43), which is dated to the late eighth or early ninth century, has three overlapping strakes trenailed on to a logboat base, extended at both ends by planking which ends in vertical boards (transoms). In contrast to the vessels depicted on the Dorestad coins, where the mast is amidships, Utrecht boat 1 has a mast step one-third of the way from the bow: this may be for a towing mast, although it has been suggested that it may have been for a mast with a fore-and-aft sail.

Another boat found at Utrecht in 1970 (number 4), generally similar to number 1, is provisionally dated to the late twelfth century, contemporary with the fonts at Winchester (fig. 44) and Zedelgem, Bruges, on which curvaceous ships are depicted. English coins (some of them excavated from a site in the Royal Naval College, Greenwich) of the fourteenth and fifteenth centuries (fig. 45) have ships of a similar shape.

Fig. 44. A scene on the late twelfth-century font in Winchester Cathedral with a ship thought to represent a *hulc*.

Fig. 45. An *angel,* a gold coin of Henry VII, excavated from a site in the Royal Naval College, Greenwich, and showing a possible *hulc.*

The town seal of New Shoreham (AD 1295) depicts a ship of this curved form and the surrounding inscription identifies it as a *hulc* (fig. 46). This type name is first known from the late tenth or early eleventh century laws of Aethelred II of England and subsequently is frequently mentioned in accounts from the twelfth to fifteenth centuries. By the thirteenth century *hulcs* were of importance to English sea-going trade, and by the fifteenth century this type seems to have taken over from the cog as the dominant sea-going ship in north-west European waters. It has been suggested that all boats and ships with this curved shape are *hulcs,* including those depicted on the Dorestad coins and

Utrecht boats 1 and 4. It is important to remember, however, that there are only two characteristics (the curved overall shape and the run of the planking) which link the examples in this suggested series. Very many more, possibly hundreds, of attributes (characteristic features) are required to describe a ship in detail: thus, not until further examples are excavated of this postulated curved hull tradition can we identify those features which define it. The link with the type name *hulc* is irrelevant to this archaeological search to define a tradition of building technology. Once this is achieved, however, the link with the type name, if valid, will allow documentary, iconographic and archaeological evidence to be integrated and a detailed description of this ship type and its activities to be made.

Fig. 46. The town seal of New Shoreham, West Sussex, of *c* AD 1295. The inscription links the depicted ship with the former name of the town, Hulkesmouth.

Inland and inshore craft

Some other boat finds from the seventh to fifteenth centuries are box-like forms from inland waterway or harbour sites from Russia to Germany. Apart from their form they differ from one another in a number of ways. It remains to be seen, therefore, whether they are members of one tradition of boatbuilding or of several, their shapes being similar because this was the best one for the function they had to perform.

Late medieval developments

By the end of the fifteenth century three-masted ships had become almost commonplace, capable of sailing all the seas of the world. But increase in sail power was not the only change: these ships were *skeleton-built,* that is, unlike the great majority of their predecessors, a skeleton of timbers was first built to a predetermined shape (the ship was 'designed', in other words) and the hull planking was fastened to it. Earlier ships had been *shell-built,* the skin of planking being first built, by eye or with the aid of simple devices, and the supporting ribs and crossbeams were inserted afterwards. Skeleton building techniques allowed bigger ships to be built which could absorb the stresses of several masts and sails and could accept gun ports through their sides. Their size allowed them to carry more cargo and to sail further without replenishment. They were the ships in which Europeans 'discovered' all the seas of the world within the space of fifty years in the late fifteenth and early sixteenth centuries. Precisely when and where this change in shipbuilding techniques took place is not yet known. The potential was there in both north-western Europe and in the Mediterranean: a fusion of ideas and techniques from these two regions may have initiated this 'revolution'. The matter is unresolved, but research is in progress.

Propulsion and steering

Paddles have been recovered from many excavations and could have been available to propel boats and rafts from very early times. A fifth-century BC gold model from Dürnberg, Germany, has the earliest evidence for the use of pivoted oars in northern Europe and 'punt' poles are known from Roman times although their earlier use is likely. Vessels can be steered as well as propelled by paddle, pole or oar; but with sails separate means of steering are required – in northern and western Europe the earliest form seems to have been a specially shaped paddle used over the quarter. Sail was in use in the Mediterranean from at least 2000 BC, but the earliest evidence for indigenous sail in north-west Europe is the mast and yard on the first-century BC Broighter boat model and Caesar's description of the sails of the Veneti. In northern Europe documentary and iconographic evidence suggests that the sail was in use on indigenous craft from at least the sixth century AD.

Most representations show a rectangular sail that is broader than it is deep, although an early Celtic sail appears to have been deeper than broad and fitted with horizontal battens and a boom. Until the last century of the medieval period the single square sail on a yard and mast stepped near amidships seems to have been the rule throughout northern and western Europe.

Landing places

Except in the classical world, boats of the prehistoric period and of the medieval period up to the tenth or eleventh century AD did not need or use formal landing places with wharfs and jetties where they might lie alongside afloat. Logboats, skinboats, plank boats and rafts used the beach or the gently sloping riverbank, or they anchored off or moored in shallow water: we see such scenes illustrated on the Bayeux Tapestry. Making a landing at such an informal site might be done by running the boat aground; the boat would be refloated either by being pushed off the beach or on a rising tide. Alternatively, in tidal conditions, boats could anchor or make fast to mooring posts or stones in the shallows and take the ground on a falling tide; or they could remain afloat so that men had to wade to and from them.

On soft muddy sites, as at the ninth-century findspot of the Graveney boat, simple hardstandings of hurdles or of horizontal poles, withies and stakes were constructed so that the boat would not stick in the mud. Such sites might also have causeways of similar hurdle construction jutting out from dry land to allow access to the shoreline across the muddy foreshore or the boggy approach to a river.

In the tenth or eleventh century AD, as towns grew and economic life became relatively complex, demand increased for low-density, mass-consumption goods: as a result sea-going ships were developed in size. These larger ships could best be loaded and discharged at deep water berths alongside wharfs; the collection of custom dues, warehouse methods of marketing and requirements to stabilise a beach or a riverbank or to enclose sea areas to gain ground reinforced this trend towards formal harbour facilities for ships.

Pilotage and navigation

The mariner's compass (lodestone) was not used in north-western waters until the twelfth century AD, astrolabes and similar instruments for determining latitude not until the fourteenth or fifteenth century, and the problem of longitude was not resolved until the eighteenth century. It seems probable that many early sea voyages were coastal ones or across channels where land was generally in sight. In such conditions *pilotage* techniques are used: seamen became familiar with landmarks that indicate their whereabouts. The sounding or depth pole appears to have been known to the ancient Egyptians and, by using this or the later leadline, the approach to shallows can be recognised; furthermore, the nature of the sea bottom determined from the lead gives a guide to position. Similarly, estuaries may be detected from seaward by a change in the flow and colour of the water. When a ship is temporarily out of sight of land contact may be regained by reference to the sun, if visible. Megalithic alignments suggest that early man in northern Europe observed the night sky. Whether any star or group of stars was used to give a rough idea of direction in the neolithic is conjectural, but it does not seem impossible. By the bronze age the significance of the North Star was certainly appreciated in the Mediterranean, and it may also have been further north.

In conditions of good visibility much of the world could have been discovered by these coastal or cross-channel voyages. But this is not so for the oceanic islands, and the Irishmen who settled in Iceland and other northern islands by the early eighth century AD necessarily must have been out of sight of land and thus *navigational* methods must have been used. The Vikings in later centuries made two-way ocean voyages to Iceland and Greenland during which they were out of sight of land for several consecutive days. Little evidence survives of the techniques they used, and the best one can now do is to examine methods known to have been used by medieval Arabs, nineteenth-century Polynesians and by recent North Sea skippers who seem to have navigated safely with the minimum of modern aids. What follows is conjectural but is not incompatible with the technology and achievements of early medieval times and may possibly have applied as far back as the bronze age.

Dead reckoning may be used to give reasonably accurate positions, the aim being to plot (possibly mentally) the best estimates of the course steered and the distance run. Course may be estimated relative to a steady swell or the prevailing wind from a known direction, or at night by reference to the Pole Star. Checks on these estimates may be made with tolerable accuracy by noting the direction of the sun at sunrise, sunset and when it is at its highest. Speed may be estimated on a particular voyage from a knowledge of past performance and existing wind and sea conditions; it may also be estimated from the position of the bow wave, or by counting the number of oar strokes used to propel the boat past a floating object thrown overboard from the bow. The effects of current and leeway may also be estimated by an experienced seaman. Much would depend on tradition and experience, on an eye for the weather and possibly on skills that we no longer realise we possess.

Approaching land may be heralded by cloud sitting over it or by the boom of surf or the flightline of seabirds. Soundings may be taken to warn of decreasing depths of water as land is neared. The shape of high peaks or the outline of a range of hills can be memorised, and in later times landmarks, beacons and high church towers were built as aids to seamen. Using these and other pilotage methods the master would be able to identify his landfall and turn along the coast for his destination.

4
Museums to visit

United Kingdom

Museum of London, London Wall, London EC2. Telephone: 01-600 3699. Display on the early craft of the river Thames, including the Blackfriars boats and the County Hall find.

National Maritime Museum, Romney Road, Greenwich, London SE10. Telephone: 01-858 4422. Displays on the Ferriby boats, the Sutton Hoo burial boat and the Graveney boat; archaeological techniques; boatbuilding tools; aspects of conservation; ethnographic craft.

National Museum of Antiquities of Scotland, Queen Street, Edinburgh. Telephone: 031-556 8921. Logboats and some medieval stems.

National Museum of Wales, Cathays Park, Cardiff. Telephone: Cardiff (0222) 397951. The Caergwrle model.

Scaplen's Court Museum, High Street, Poole, Dorset. Telephone: Poole (020 13) 5151. The Poole logboat under conservation.

Other countries

Deutches Schiffahrtsmuseum, Bremerhaven, West Germany. The Bremen cog, logboats and recent German boats.

Ijsselmeerpolders Museum, Ketelhaven, Flevoland, Netherlands. Roman age and medieval craft excavated from the river Rhine and from the reclaimed Zuyder Zee.

National Museum of Ireland, Kildare Street, Dublin. The Broighter boat model.

Schleswig-Holstein Landesmuseum, Schloss Gottorp, Schleswig, West Germany. The Nydam boat and two logboats.

Viking Ship Hall, Bigdöy, Norway. Gokstad, Oseberg and Tune finds and the small boats.

Viking Ship Barrow, Ladby, Fyn, Denmark. The Ladby boat grave preserved.

Viking Ship Museum, Roskilde, Denmark. The Skuldelev finds and other medieval craft; ethnographic boats.

Other museums with logboats

The following additional British museums have logboats either on display or in their reserve collections:

Botanic Gardens Museum, Churchtown, Southport, Merseyside. Telephone: Southport (0704) 27547.

Brecknock Museum, Captain's Walk, Brecon, Powys. Telephone: Brecon (0874) 4121.

Chelmsford and Essex Museum, Oaklands Park, Moulsham Street, Chelmsford, Essex. Telephone: Chelmsford (0245) 353066 or 60614.

Dick Institute Museum, Elmbank Avenue, Kilmarnock, Ayrshire. Telephone: Kilmarnock (0563) 26401.

Dorman Museum, Linthorpe Road, Middlesborough, Cleveland. Telephone: Middlesborough (0642) 813781/2.

Dumfries Museum, The Observatory, Church Street, Dumfries. Telephone: Dumfries (0387) 3374.

Dundee Central Museum and Art Gallery, Albert Square, Dundee. Telephone: Dundee (0382) 25492/3.

Glasgow Art Gallery and Museum, Kelvingrove, Glasgow. Telephone: 041-334 1134.

Grosvenor Museum, 27 Grosvenor Street, Chester. Telephone: Chester (0244) 21616 or 313858.

Harris Museum and Art Gallery, Market Square, Preston, Lancashire. Telephone: Preston (0772) 58248.

Hull Transport and Archaeology Museum, 36 High Street, Hull. Telephone: Hull (0482) 222737.

Hunterian Museum, University of Glasgow, Glasgow. Telephone: 041-339 8855 (extension 285).

Ipswich Museum, High Street, Ipswich, Suffolk. Telephone: Ipswich (0473) 213761.

Lincoln City and County Museum, Broadgate, Lincoln. Telephone: Lincoln (0522) 30401.

Llandrindod Wells Museum, Temple Street, Llandrindod Wells, Powys. Telephone: Llandrindod Wells (0597) 2212.

Merseyside Maritime Museum, Pier Head, Liverpool. Telephone: 051-236 1492.

Museum of Sussex Archaeology, Barbican House, High Street, Lewes, East Sussex. Telephone: Lewes (079 16) 4379.

Nottingham Castle Museum, The Castle, Nottingham. Telephone: Nottingham (0602) 411881.

Rowley's House Museum, Barker Street, Shrewsbury, Shropshire. Telephone: Shrewsbury (0743) 54811.

Scunthorpe Borough Museum and Art Gallery, Oswald Road, Scunthorpe, South Humberside. Telephone: Scunthorpe (0724) 843533.

Somerset County Museum, Taunton Castle, Castle Green, Taunton, Somerset. Telephone: Taunton (0823) 3451 (extension 286).

Sunderland Museum and Art Gallery, Borough Road, Sunderland, Tyne and Wear. Telephone: Sunderland (0783) 41235.

West Highland Museum, Cameron Square, Fort William, Inverness-shire. Telephone: Fort William (0397) 2169.

Weybridge Museum, Church Street, Weybridge, Surrey. Telephone: Weybridge (0932) 43573.

Worthing Museum and Art Gallery, Chapel Road, Worthing, West Sussex. Telephone: Worthing (0903) 39999 (extension 121).

5
Further reading

Bass, G. (editor). *History of Seafaring.* Thames and Hudson, 1972.

Greenhill, B. *Archaeology of the Boat.* A. and C. Black, 1976.

Hornell, J. *Water Transport.* David and Charles, 1970.

Johnstone, P. *Seacraft of Prehistory.* Routledge and Kegan Paul, 1980.

McGrail, S. *Rafts, Boats and Ships.* HMSO, 1981.

Muckelroy, K. *Maritime Archaeology.* Cambridge University Press, 1978.

International Journal of Nautical Archaeology: obtainable from the Nautical Archaeology Society, c/o Mrs V. Fenwick, 1 Old Hall, South Grove, Highgate Village, London N6 6BP.

Mariners' Mirror: obtainable from the Society for Nautical Research, c/o National Maritime Museum, Greenwich, London SE10 9NF.

The National Maritime Museum publishes Maritime Monographs and a series of archaeological books.

64

Index

Page numbers in italic refer to illustrations